FUN WITH SCIENCE

WATER

BRENDA WALPOLE

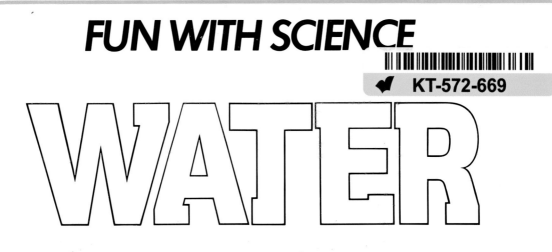

Contents

Use the symbols below to help you
identify the three kinds of practical
activities in this book.

EXPERIMENTS   TRICKS   THINGS TO MAKE

Illustrated by Kuo Kang Chen · Peter Bull

Introduction

Water is a remarkable substance. It covers more than two-thirds of the Earth's surface and no life on Earth could survive without it. Most of the experiments in this book will help you to investigate the amazing characteristics of liquid water. You can take a close look at water's stretchy 'skin', discover why heavy ships float in water and find out how some substances disappear when they are mixed with water. You can also find out how liquid water is used to turn the machinery that produces the electricity in hydro-electric power stations.

But liquid water is only one of the three forms in which water can exist. If water is cooled to 0°C, it freezes to become a solid called ice. If it is heated to 100°C, it boils and disappears into the air as a gas called water vapour.

As you come to understand the different characteristics of water you will be able to answer the questions on these two pages and explain how water influences the way in which things happen in the world around you.

This book covers six main topics:

- Water as a liquid, a solid and a gas
- Water levels and flowing water
- Surface tension
- Density and displacement
- Dissolving substances in water
- Water for life and power

A blue line (like the one around the edge of these two pages) indicates the start of a new topic.

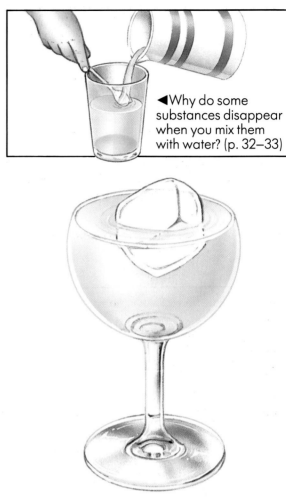

◀Why do some substances disappear when you mix them with water? (p. 32–33)

▲Why does an ice cube float in water and an iceberg float in the sea? (pages 8–9)

▼ Why do some objects float and others sink? (pages 24–25)

▲ What makes clouds form in the sky?
Why are clouds different shapes? (pages 6–7)

▶ How does soap
clean greasy dishes?
(pages 22–23)

▼ Why does water always
settle on a horizontal level?
(pages 12–13)

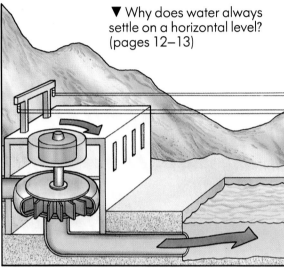

◀ How fast can water
flow? (pages 16–17)

▲ How is water used to produce electricity?
(pages 38–39)

▶ Where do snow and ice come from?
(pages 8–9)

▼ Why do ships float in water?
How much cargo can they hold? (pages 26–27)

Disappearing Water

When it rains, water falls from the sky and collects in puddles on the ground. But after the rain has stopped and the Sun begins to shine, the puddles dry up and the water disappears. Where does all the water go? The heat of the Sun makes the water turn into tiny droplets, which rise up into the air. This process is called **evaporation** and the droplets are called **water vapour**.

►In hot countries, fruit is left out in the Sun to dry. The water in the fruit slowly turns into water vapour and evaporates into the air. This helps to preserve the fruit so it can be stored and used later.

Investigate Evaporation

Equipment: Two jars (the same shape and size), tin foil, a marker pen.

1. Fill the two jars about half full of water. Check the water level is the same in both jars and mark the level on the outside.
2. Make a foil cover for one of the jars.
3. Leave both jars in a warm place for a few days. Then check the water levels again. Which jar has less water in it?

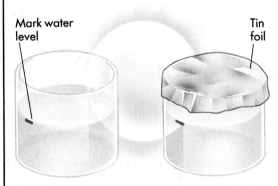

Mark water level

Tin foil

How it works
The heat makes the water evaporate in both jars. But the foil cover stops the water vapour escaping into the air so the level of water remains higher in this jar.

Drying the Washing

How quickly does water evaporate from objects and make them dry out? Try these investigations to find the best drying conditions.

Cut a piece of cloth into six pieces – make them all about the same size. Wet all the cloths.
● Put one in the sun and one in the shade.
● Hang one in a breeze and one in still air.
● Leave one folded or squashed into a ball and spread one out flat.
Which piece of cloth dries first?

Make Your Own Refrigerator

One way to keep things cool is to cover them with a clay pot (such as a tall flower pot), which you have soaked in water. As water evaporates from the clay pot it takes heat away so the object underneath will remain cool. If you stand the pot in a bowl of water, it will soak up more water as it dries out and your 'fridge' will last longer.

Stone ——

Clay pot ——

Cool drink ——

Water evaporates most rapidly in a warm, sunny place. A breeze carries away the water vapour that evaporates from the surface of the cloth and this helps the cloth to dry. Spreading out the cloth also makes it dry faster as water can evaporate from the whole surface. So the best time to dry the washing is in warm, windy weather and the clothes will dry faster if they are spread out.

More things to try
Compare different materials, such as artificial and natural fabrics. Put them in the same place and see which one of them dries first.

Keeping Cool

Why do you feel cold when you get out of a warm bath? This is because water evaporates from your skin and takes heat away with it. The same process helps you to cool down if you get very hot, for example if you run in a race. Sweat escapes from pores in your skin and evaporates to cool you down.

Water from Air

Water vapour does not always stay in the air. It sometimes turns back into liquid water again. This is called **condensation** and it happens when air cools down. Cold air cannot hold as much water vapour as warm air so some of the water vapour condenses to form tiny drops of liquid water. The white trails made by high-flying aircraft are formed as a result of condensation.

Making Water Appear

Put a glass of water in the refrigerator for an hour or so until it is quite cold. When you take it out, you will see drops of water forming on the sides of the glass.

How it works
The cold glass cools the air around it and some of the water vapour condenses to form drops of water on the sides of the glass. This is why you may see water droplets running down the inside of misty window panes on cold days.

What is Steam?

The steam from a boiling kettle forms as water vapour escapes from the hot water inside and meets the colder air outside. Tiny drops of liquid water condense from the vapour and join together until they are big enough for you to see as clouds of steam.

Wear an oven glove to hold the spoon.

If you hold a cold spoon in the steam, the water vapour will condense and drip off.
Warning: Take care; steam is very hot and could burn you.

Why Does it Rain?

Heat from the Sun makes the liquid water in oceans, rivers and lakes evaporate and water vapour rises into the air. At very high levels, the air is too cold to hold all the vapour.

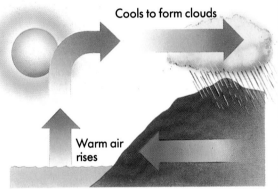

Cools to form clouds

Warm air rises

Clouds begin to form as the water vapour condenses in the cold air to form drops of water. The drops stay in the clouds until they get too heavy to hang in the air. When that happens, they fall as rain.

Heap clouds

Wispy clouds

Layer clouds

Look out for three main cloud shapes. Fluffy, heap clouds (cumulus) mean fine weather but may grow into huge, grey storm clouds later on. Layer clouds (stratus) bring rain or snow. Wispy clouds (cirrus) are so high they are made of ice crystals.

Make a Rain Gauge

All you need to measure the rainfall in your area is a clear plastic bottle and a ruler. Cut the top off the bottle and fit it upside down into the rest of the bottle to form a funnel. Use the ruler to mark a scale on the side of the bottle.

Set up your rain gauge in an open place – not under trees where drops of water from the trees might fall in. Fix it firmly in the ground and keep it out of the wind so that it is not blown over and the wind does not blow the raindrops away from the funnel.

Check the amount of rain that falls each day and make your own rainfall chart. Remember to empty the bottle each day after you have filled in your chart.

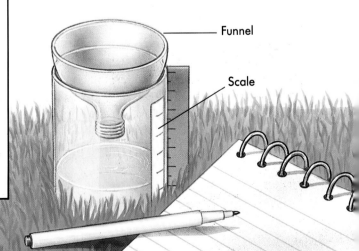

Funnel

Scale

Frozen Solid

Water is a remarkable substance because it can exist in three different forms – as a liquid, as a gas (water vapour) and as a solid (ice). On the next four pages, you can find out more about solid water and how to use its special properties in some simple tricks and experiments. Solid water can form in two ways. The first is when liquid water cools to 0°C (32°F) – its 'freezing point'. This is how ice cubes form. The second is when water vapour freezes – this is how the 'frost' forms in a freezer.

Floating Ice

As water freezes and changes to ice, it expands and takes up more space than it did as liquid water. This makes the ice lighter than the liquid water it was made from and so it floats – but only just. Because ice takes up about one ninth more space than it does as liquid water, about one ninth of an iceberg shows above the water. There is nine times as much below the surface.

The hidden part of an iceberg is dangerous to ships.

Looking for Ice

During the winter, look for the different shapes and patterns that frozen water can make.
- Snowflakes form when water vapour freezes.
- Icicles form when water drips in very cold air.
- Ice crystals make patterns on cold window panes when water vapour freezes slowly.
- Sheets of ice cover the surfaces of puddles, pails, tubs and ponds.

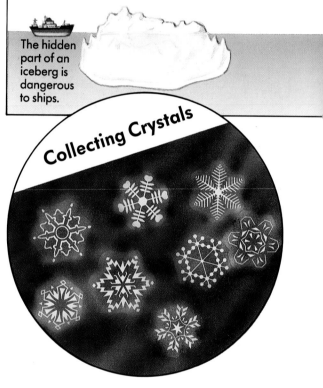

Collecting Crystals

Catch snowflakes on a piece of black cloth or card that has been kept in a refrigerator – this helps to stop the snowflakes melting. Use a magnifying glass to examine them. Each one is different but they all have six sides!

 **Ice Needs Space**

Float an ice cube in a glass of water. What do you think will happen when the ice cube melts? Will the glass overflow?

When the ice cube melts, the level of water in the glass stays about the same. This is because the water from the ice takes up less space than the ice itself.

Equipment: A small bottle made of glass or thick plastic – about the same size as the bottles used for food colouring.

1. Fill the bottle to the brim with water and make a loose-fitting cap out of tin foil. Put the bottle in the freezer and leave it until the water has frozen hard.

2. When you look at it again, you will see that the ice has pushed up the cap.

How it works
Ice takes up more space than the water that froze to make it. This is why pipes may burst in winter. The water inside them expands as it freezes and forces the joints apart or makes the pipes split.

Cut Ice With String

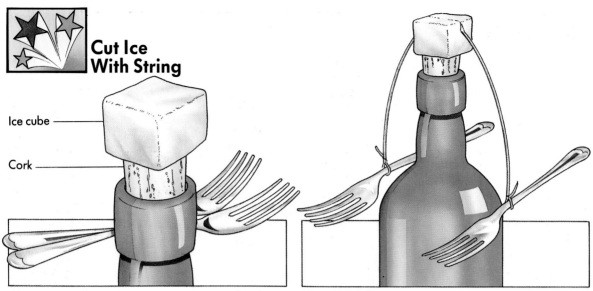

Ice cube

Cork

Equipment: Thin, strong string or wire, a bottle with a cork, a cube of ice, two heavy forks.

1. Push the cork into the bottle so that about 2.5 cm (1 inch) sticks out. Balance the ice cube on top of the cork.

2. Cut a piece of string or wire about 40 cm (1 foot 4 inches) long and tie one fork to each end. Hang the string over the ice cube. Put the bottle in the refrigerator. The string will pass through the ice without dividing it into two.

How it works

The pressure of the string or wire makes the ice melt just below it. Water forms under the string or wire and it slides down through the ice. The ice freezes again just above the string or wire.

This is what happens when people skate on ice. Their weight presses on the ice and makes it melt under the blades of the skates. The layer of water helps the skates to glide over the ice. The water freezes again afterwards.

Houses of Ice

The Inuit (Eskimo) people of Canada used to build houses out of ice to live in when they went on hunting trips, These houses (called igloos) were built from blocks of frozen snow, which were placed on top of each other to make a dome-shaped hut. The gaps between the blocks were filled with loose snow and a hole was left in the top for air to get in and out. Heat from a stove inside made the walls begin to melt. Opening the door made this liquid water freeze to form a layer of ice, which stopped heat escaping.

Today, very few Inuit build traditional igloos or make long hunting journeys across the ice.

Lift Ice With a Matchstick

Equipment: A bowl of water, an ice cube, a matchstick, some salt.

Float the ice cube in the bowl of water and lay the matchstick carefully on the top of the cube. Then sprinkle a little salt around the matchstick. Soon it will be frozen into the ice cube and you will be able to use the matchstick to lift the ice.

How it works

When you sprinkle salt onto the ice cube, it makes the ice around the matchstick melt. This is because salt water freezes at a lower temperature than ordinary water. In other words, it has to get colder than 0°C (32°F) before salt water will freeze. But no salt falls under the matchstick and it becomes frozen into the ice. This allows you to lift the ice with the matchstick.

Salt is spread on roads in the winter to melt the ice. The salty water that is left does not freeze until the temperature is well below 0°C. Adding anti-freeze to the water in car radiators is another way to stop water freezing. A mixture of the two liquids will not freeze until minus 30°C (minus 22°F).

On the Level

Water (and everything else on Earth) is pulled towards the centre of the Earth by an invisible force called **gravity**. In some places, the water gets no further than the surface because certain types of rock stop it from draining through. This water forms rivers, lakes and oceans. In other places, different types of rock let the water soak through. All water on Earth eventually settles at the lowest level it can possibly reach.

▲ Waterfalls provide spectacular evidence of how water is pulled down to Earth and always finds its own level. This photograph shows Niagara Falls, which is on the border between the USA and Canada.

Guess the Level

All you need is paper, pencil and scissors.
1. Fold a large sheet of paper in half and then in half again.
2. Draw a bottle shape on one side and cut it out through all four thicknesses of paper.

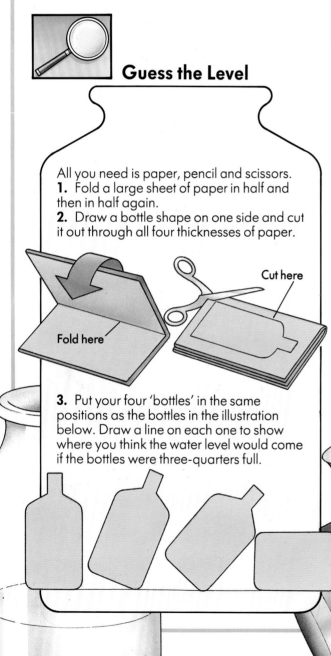

Cut here

Fold here

3. Put your four 'bottles' in the same positions as the bottles in the illustration below. Draw a line on each one to show where you think the water level would come if the bottles were three-quarters full.

4. Then repeat the experiment with a real bottle of water. (Make sure you hold it over a bath or go outside when you tip it up.) Did you guess the water levels correctly?

The surface of the water in any container is always horizontal – however much you tip the container. Try this for yourself using containers like those in the illustration below.

Make Water Flow Upwards

Place one empty bowl on a surface that is lower than the other bowl. Fill the higher bowl with water. Put a finger over one end of the plastic tube and fill it with water. Put the end with your finger over it under the surface of the water in the higher bowl and place the other end in the empty bowl. When you take your finger away, you should see the water flow **up** the tube, out of the higher bowl and down into the other bowl.

How it works
The tube forms a **siphon**, which works because air presses on the surface of the water in the higher bowl and forces water **up** the tube.

This experiment shows you how to make water defy the laws of gravity and flow upwards!
Equipment: Large bowls and plastic tubing.

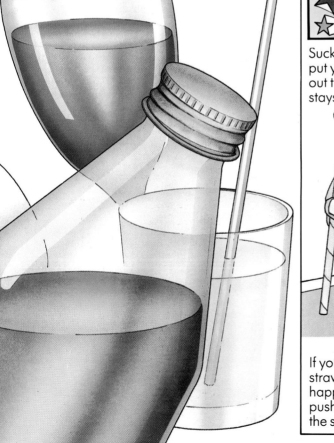

The Impossible Straw

Suck some water up into a straw. Quickly put your finger over the top end and hold out the straw – keep it upright. All the water stays in the straw!

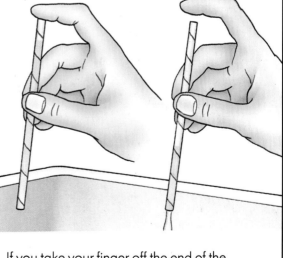

If you take your finger off the end of the straw, the water flows out. This cannot happen unless air can get in at the top to push down on the water and force it out of the straw.

Moving Upwards

On these two pages are some more ways of overcoming the pull of gravity and making water flow upwards. Some of the experiments use air pressure or heat to make the water rise. Others make use of the fact that the water in narrow tubes tends to be pulled upwards by means of a process called **capillary action**.

Colour a Flower

1. Cut about 5 cm (2 inches) off the bottom of a flower stem.
2. Put several drops of colouring in a vase of water.
3. Stand the flower in the water for several hours. Eventually the petals will begin to turn the colour of the water in the vase.

Lift Water in a Glass

Put a glass under the surface of the water in a bowl. Turn it upside down.

Lift it slowly but don't let the rim of the glass come above the surface of the water. What happens?

Then try lifting the glass above the surface of the water. Now what happens?

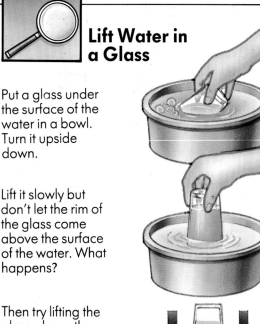

How it works
Air presses down on the surface of the water and pushes some of the water up into the glass. But when the rim of the glass comes above the surface, the air no longer supports the water and it falls out of the glass.

Underwater Volcano

Equipment: A small bottle, a large glass jar full of water, string, food colouring or ink.

1. Tie the string round the neck of the bottle.
2. Fill the bottle with hot water and add one or two drops of colouring or ink.

3. Carefully lower the small bottle into the large jar. Watch as the coloured water rises upwards, like a volcano.

How it works
The hot water is lighter than the cold water so it rises and floats to the top of the jar. Later, as the hot water cools, it will mix evenly with the cold water and all the water will become the same colour.

Equipment: A freshly cut flower (such as a carnation or daffodil), a vase of water, food colouring or ink.

How it works
The flower 'sucks up' the coloured water through narrow tubes in its stem. The pull of this **capillary action** is enough to overcome the pull of gravity.

More things to try
You can make flowers of more than one colour by splitting the stem in half and standing each half in different coloured water.

Open a Flower

Equipment: Smooth (but not shiny) paper, pencils, scissors, a bowl of water.

Draw a flower shape like this on your paper and colour it in if you like.

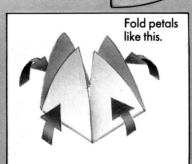

Fold petals like this.

Cut out the flower and fold the petals down flat. When you float the flower on the water, the petals will slowly open as a result of capillary action.

Water gradually rises up through tiny, tube-like holes between the fibres of the paper. The paper swells and the petals open up, just like a real flower.

Flowing Water

The speed at which water flows downwards is controlled by the pull of gravity and the shape of the land. But if water is put under pressure it flows more quickly.

Make a Water Clock

Thousands of years ago, the Chinese and the Egyptians used flowing water to measure time. You can make a water clock similar to the ones they used.

Equipment: A long ruler, two identical yoghurt cartons or disposable coffee cups, strong, sticky tape, a small nail, modelling clay.
1. Use the nail to make a small hole in the middle of the bottom of one of the containers. Mark a scale on the inside of the other container.
2. Fix the containers to the ruler using sticky tape. Put the container marked with the scale at the bottom. Stand the ruler upright by fixing the end in modelling clay.

Time how long it takes for the water to reach each one of the levels on your scale.

3. Cover the hole in the top container with your finger and fill it with water. Then take away your finger and time how long it takes for the water to reach each of the levels in the other container. Can you make a clock that times periods of one minute accurately?

Water and Other Liquids

Investigate how fast water flows compared to other liquids. Prepare two containers in the same way as for the water clock (above). Time how long water takes to drip from one container to another. Then try other liquids, such as treacle, cooking oil or fruit syrup. Which liquid flows fastest?

▼ A model of a Chinese water clock. The wheel moves round each time a bucket fills with water and makes 100 complete turns in 24 hours.

◄ Fire hoses use water that is under high pressure. This makes the water shoot out of the hose in a fast-flowing stream so that a lot of water reaches the fire quickly.

Use a drawing pin or nail to make the holes. They must all be the same size.

Water Power

You can make water flow more quickly by squashing it into a smaller space or by making the water deeper so it puts itself under pressure.

Find an empty washing-up liquid bottle. Take off the cap and fill the bottle with water. Then put the cap back on. Over the bath or out of doors, try squeezing the bottle gently. Then try squeezing it hard. As you press the water into a smaller space, the water will flow faster.

Now empty the bottle again and make three holes in the side. Cover the holes with your fingers and fill the bottle with water. Take away your fingers and see which hole produces the longest jet of water.

How it works
The water at the bottom of the bottle is pushed down by all the water above it so the hole at the bottom produces a long jet of fast flowing water. The other jets are shorter.

A Stretchy Skin

Take a good look at raindrops or the drops of water falling from a tap. What shape are the water drops? You should see that the smallest drops are nearly perfect spheres. This is because the surface of the water is held together by a strong force called **surface tension**, which makes the water look as if it has a thin, elastic 'skin' all over it.

Curving Water

Carefully fill a cup or glass with water right to the brim. You will be able to see how surface tension pulls the surface of the water together so it curves above the rim of the container.

Find some dry brushes – a small paint brush and a shaving brush are good ones to try. Look at the shape of the bristles, then dip them in water. You will see that the bristles are pulled together to form a point at the tip of the brushes. Surface tension is strong enough to pull in the bristles and the water.

The Water Walkers

Some insects, such as pond skaters, can walk on water without sinking in. The 'skin' on the surface is strong enough to support them. It bends a little to form small dents around their feet but does not give way. The pond skaters stretch out their long legs to spread their weight over the surface 'skin'.

Float the Needle

Can you make metal float on water?

Equipment: A **clean** bowl, a fork, a needle.

1. Fill the bowl with fresh water.

2. Rest the needle across the prongs (tines) of the fork and gently break the surface of the water with the fork. If you are careful, the needle will float off as you take the fork away.

How it works

The fork breaks the 'skin' on the surface of the water but it quickly forms again under the needle. The 'skin' supports the needle and stops it from sinking. If you look closely, you may be able to see the 'skin' bending under the weight of the needle.

Keep the Water Out

Is your handkerchief waterproof? You may be surprised by this trick.

1. Fill a jar with water and soak your handkerchief.

2. Stretch the handkerchief over the mouth of of the jar and hold it in place with string or an elastic band.

3. Turn the jar upside down. Does the water pour out?

How it works

The handkerchief is made of fibres of cloth with tiny holes in between them. Surface tension acts like a 'skin' and stops water pushing down through the holes. Umbrellas stop water getting through for the same reason. Next time you are sheltering under one, think of surface tension.

Pour Water Down a String

Water flowing out of a tap in a steady stream forms a smooth tube. Surface tension keeps the water in this shape. Try pouring water down a string to see this effect for yourself.

Equipment: A small jug, string, an empty container.

1. Tie one end of the string to the handle of the jug. Fill the jug with water.
2. Pass the string over the lip of the jug and hold the free end against the inside of the container.
3. Separate the jug and the container so the string is pulled tight.
4. Hold the jug right above the container and pour slowly and carefully. The water should flow down the string into the container.
5. After the flow has started, move the jug down so it is at an angle. Surface tension should hold the water close to the string so it flows along it.

Tie string to handle of jug.

Tie Water in Knots

1. Use a nail to make 5 even holes near the bottom of a plastic container. The holes should be about 0.5 cm (¼ inch) apart.

2. Hold the container under a tap in a sink and fill it with water. You will see 5 streams of water coming out.

3. Pinch the 5 streams of water together with your fingers. You should be able to knot the streams of water together using the pull of surface tension.

4. If you brush your hand across the holes, you should be able to separate the streams of water again.

Break the Tension

Surface tension can cause unexpected things to happen. It can support objects that look as if they should sink.

Equipment: A bowl of water, a plastic basket (similar to the one in the illustration below).

1. Fill the bowl with water and gently lower the basket on to the surface. The basket should float – even though it is full of holes!

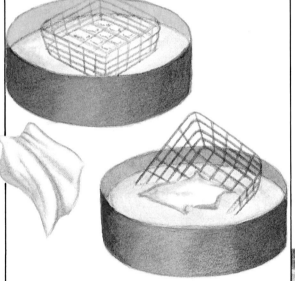

2. Now take a small piece of tissue and drop it lightly into the basket. The tissue slowly soaks up water and the basket should suddenly sink.

How it works
The basket floats because surface tension acts like a 'skin' and stops water pushing up through the holes. But when the tissue soaks up water, it breaks the 'skin' and the surface of the water cannot support the basket.

Stretching the Skin

What happens when the pull of surface tension is weakened? How stretchy is water's 'skin'?

1. Choose a large, clean plate and rinse it well.
2. Fill the plate with water and wait until the surface is smooth and still. Then sprinkle talcum powder over the surface.

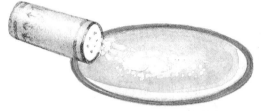

3. Wet one finger and rub it over a piece of soap. Then dip your finger in the water at one side of the plate. All the talcum will be drawn immediately to the other side of the plate.

How it works
Soap weakens the pull of surface tension in the water around your finger. The pull from the opposite side of the plate is stronger and the talcum powder is drawn over there.

Soap Power

Soap weakens the surface tension that makes the 'skin' form on the surface of water. This stretches the 'skin' and makes it possible to blow bubbles. It also makes enough pulling power to drive small boats. On these two pages are some tricks to try and things to make using this soap power.

Soap Boats

Equipment: Card or wood, scissors, small pieces of soap, bowl of water.

1. Make a boat shape out of card or wood and cut a notch in the middle at the back. Fix a tiny piece of soap in the notch.

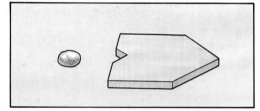

2. Fill a **clean** bowl or wash basin with water and let the water settle. Put your boat on the water and watch it move.

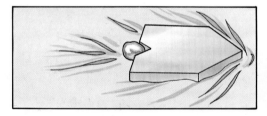

How it works
The soap weakens the surface tension behind the boat and it is pulled forward by the stronger surface tension in front.

More things to try
● Make the notch for the soap to one side of the back of the boat – what happens?
● Try adding a rudder of paperclips to steer the boat.

Magic Matchsticks

Equipment: Matches, bowl of **clean** water, soap, lump of sugar.

1. Carefully lay the matches on the surface of the water.

2. Dip the sugar lump in the middle of the bowl. The matches should move towards the sugar.

3. Now dip the soap in the middle of the bowl. The matches should move away from the soap.

How it works
When you put the sugar lump in the middle of the bowl, it absorbs some of the water. A small current of water flows towards the sugar and pulls the matches with it. But when you hold the soap in the middle of the bowl, the stronger surface tension around the edge of the bowl pulls the matches outwards.

Blowing Bubbles

You can see just how stretchy the 'skin' on the surface of water can be by blowing bubbles. You can buy bubble mixtures with a wand or you can make your own.

Bubble Recipe

Put three or four tablespoons of soap powder or soap flakes into four cups of hot water. Let the mixture stand for three days and then stir in a large spoonful of sugar. This gives extra strong bubbles.

Bubble Blowers

You can make a bubble blower by bending a piece of fuse wire (or other thin wire) into a circle. Dip your bubble blower into the soap mixture and blow through it very gently. The 'skin' will stretch and eventually a bubble will break free.

Try to find out . . .
● Are the bubbles all the same shape?
● How big can the bubbles be?
● How long do they last?
● What makes them pop?

Crystal Bubbles

Take your bubble blower and soap mixture outside when it is very cold and there is no wind. Use a round bubble blower and gently blow a large bubble. Do not let the bubble blow away and hold it still. If it is very cold, the thin bubble should begin to freeze as you watch. You should be able to see tiny crystals forming over the surface of the bubble until it freezes completely. Then you will have a very thin ice crystal ball.

More things to try
● Bend the wire into a square or triangle – What happens to the bubbles?
● Use a drinking straw instead of the wire. Make four slits about 1 cm (½ inch) from the end of the straw.
● Blow enormous bubbles by dipping your hand in the bubble mixture and blowing through a ring made with your thumb and first finger.

Floating and Sinking

Why do some objects float and others sink? Do large objects float more easily than small ones? Does the shape of an object make any difference? Try these experiments to find out.

Will it Float on Water?

Choose several solid objects – make sure they are not hollow. Guess which ones will float and then test them in a bowl of water or in the bath.

Objects to test: A stone, an orange, an apple, a screw, pieces of wood, an egg, coins, polystyrene, pumice stone, candle, seeds, erasers.

How it works

Water tries to support solid objects. If the objects are heavy for their size, they will sink; if they are light for their size, they will float. An object that is heavy for its size is said to have a high **density**. An empty lift has a low density but as it begins to fill with people, its density increases. Its size stays the same, however. This is why objects that are the same size can have different densities. A brick is more dense than a piece of wood of the same size because the stony particles that make up the brick are heavy and packed more tightly together than the fibres in the block of wood.

Density

Density is how heavy something is compared to its volume. You can work out the density of an object by dividing its weight by its volume. One cubic centimetre of water weighs one gram, so water has a density of one. If an object has a density greater than one, it will sink in water. If an object has a density of less than one, it will float on water.

Does Wood Float?

When you investigated floating and sinking, you probably found that pieces of wood float easily. But did you know that some types of wood sink in water? Pieces of cork (the bark of cork trees) and maple float easily but mahogany is only just supported by water. Ebony (the hard, black wood sometimes used to make piano keys) does not float at all because it is more dense than water.

Cork   Maple   Mahogany   Ebony

More things to try

Now that you have tested solid floaters and sinkers, mould a ball of modelling clay into different shapes and see if they float. Use the same amount of clay each time. Here are a few shapes to try:

A solid ball of modelling clay will sink straight to the bottom. But if you make it into a boat shape with high sides, it will float. So the shape of floaters and sinkers **is** important. Turn over to find out more . . .

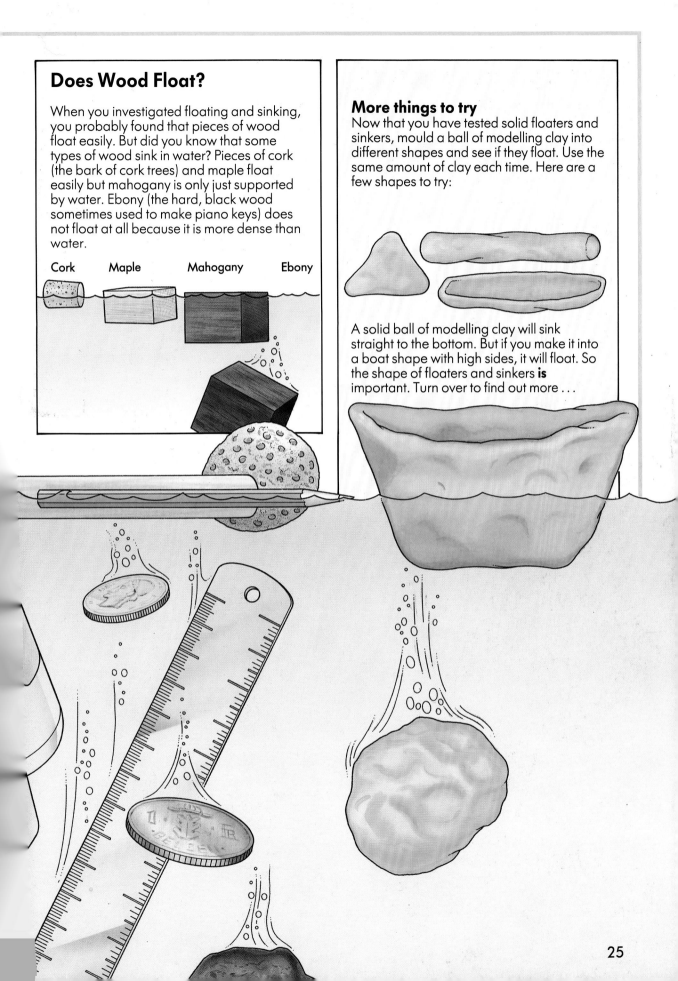

Pushing Water Out of the Way

Both the density (p.24–25) and the shape of an object affect whether it will float or sink in water. The shape of an object controls the amount of water that it pushes out of the way or '**displaces**'. If the amount of water that is displaced weighs more than the object, it will float. If the displaced water weighs less than the object, it will sink.

▶ A large ship floats because it displaces a lot of water. Even though the ship is heavy, it still weighs less than the amount of water it displaces.

Experiment With Size and Shape

Try lifting something heavy (such as a full tin) underwater and then lift the same object in air. You will find that things are much lighter and easier to lift under the water. This is because the water pushes up under the objects and tries to support them. But how much less do they weigh? Objects that are completely underwater lose the same weight as the weight of water they displace.

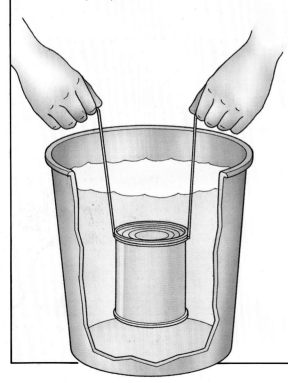

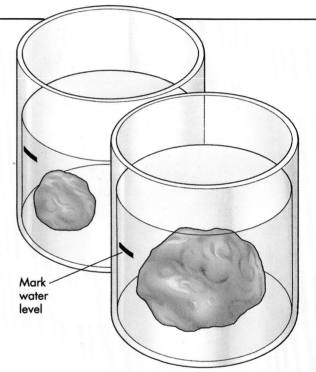

Mark water level

The amount of water that an object pushes out of the way or 'displaces' depends partly on its size. Large objects displace more water.

Fill a jar with water and mark the level. Drop in a ball of modelling clay and see how the level rises. Then try a much larger ball and see how much more the level rises.

Ships may sink if they are overloaded so all ships have a mark like this on the side. It tells the captain how low the ship can float in the water without sinking.

This mark is called the Plimsoll line after its inventor, Samuel Plimsoll.

Bowl of modelling clay

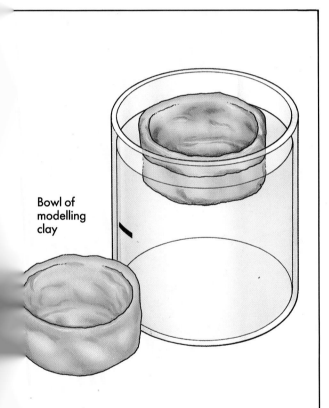

As well as size, the amount of water displaced by an object has a lot to do with its shape.

Change the shape of your piece of modelling clay to make a bowl. When you float the bowl in the jar, you will see that far more water is pushed out of the way and the level of water in the jar will be higher than before. Both the bowl and the air inside it push water out of the way.

Loading the Boat

Make a boat out of modelling clay or paper or use a toy boat. Float the boat in the water and mark the water level on the side. Load your boat with small items, such as paper clips. Add a few at a time and watch your boat float lower and lower in the water. How much cargo will your boat carry before it sinks? This is how the Plimsoll line works (see above).

27

Make a Pen-top Diver

This fascinating toy works in a similar way to a submarine by displacing water to make it dive and re-surface.

Equipment: A tall bottle, a pen-top, modelling clay or paperclips, string or an elastic band and a thin rubber sheet.

1. Fill the bottle to the brim with water. Add the modelling clay or paperclips to make the pen-top heavier until it **just** floats and is on the point of sinking. (You can fix the paperclips with fine thread or make a hole in the pen-top to loop them through.) Take plenty of time to get this right.

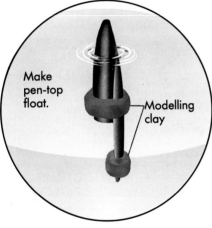

Make pen-top float.

Modelling clay

How it works
Plastic is only a little heavier than water. A bubble of air is trapped inside the pen-top and this is enough to make it float. When you press down on the rubber lid, you squeeze the tiny air bubble into a smaller space so more water can get inside the pen-top. This make the pen-top heavier so it sinks. When you stop pressing, the air can expand and push out the extra water so the pen-top rises.

More things to try
Make another sort of diver using orange peel – you could cut out a boat shape from the peel. The peel contains tiny bubbles of air so it will sink and rise in the same way as the pen-top. You will find it always floats with the orange side down because the orange part of the peel is heavier.

How a Submarine Works

Submarines use the principle of displacement to enable them to dive and come up to the surface again. At the surface, submarines float in the same way as ordinary ships. But they have special tanks inside them that can be filled with air or water to change the weight of the submarine. You can see how this works for yourself if you float a bottle full of air and gradually allow it to fill with water.

2. Stretch the sheet of rubber over the mouth of the bottle and hold it in place with string or the elastic band. Press down on the rubber with the palm of your hand and your 'diver' will go down! When you take your hand away, it will rise again.

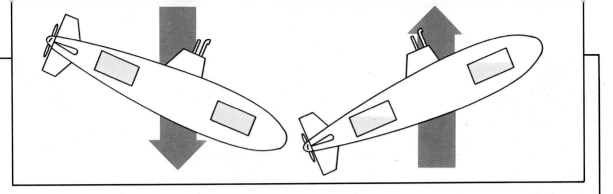

When the submarine is ready to dive, the tanks are flooded with sea water. This makes the submarine heavier than the water it displaces, so it sinks.

To return to the surface, compressed air is pumped into the tanks. This forces out the sea water and makes the submarine lighter than the water it displaces, so it floats again.

Bouncing Moth Balls

Equipment: A glass jar or vase, moth balls, vinegar, bicarbonate of soda.

1. Fill the glass jar with water. Stir in about ⅓ cup of vinegar and two teaspoons of bicarbonate of soda. Stir slowly and carefully so the mixture does not froth up too much.

2. Drop a few moth balls into the fizzy liquid. At first they will sink to the bottom but after a little while each one will rise to the surface again. But they will not stay there! They will keep sinking to the bottom and bouncing up again for several hours.

How it works
The bubbles are a gas called carbon dioxide, which is formed when the vinegar and bicarbonate of soda join together in a chemical reaction. (This is the same gas that makes the bubbles in fizzy drinks.) If you look carefully at the moth balls, you will see that they collect bubbles when they are on the bottom. The bubbles are lighter than water and they lift the moth balls up to the surface. But lots of the bubbles escape into the air and the moth balls become too heavy for the few remaining bubbles to support them — so they sink again. On the bottom, they soon collect more bubbles and bounce up again.

Hint
If the moth balls are too smooth, the bubbles cannot hold on, so the trick will not work. Rub the moth balls with sandpaper to make the surface rough.

Liquid Layers

It is not only solid things that either float or sink in water. Different liquids also have different **densities** (see pages 24–25), which means that some are heavier than others. If a liquid does not mix with water, it is possible to find out if it is more or less dense than water.

▶ This boat is spraying an oil slick, which is floating on the surface of the sea. The spray makes the oil sink to the bottom so it does not float towards land and pollute the beaches.

Find the Density

Equipment: Water, syrup, cooking oil (about a cup of each), a tall glass jar, a jug.

Pour the liquids carefully into the glass jar one after the other. You will see that they separate into three layers – the syrup sinks below the water and the oil floats on top.
Which liquid has the highest density?

Try floating some objects on your liquid layers. Things you might try include: a piece of candle, a cork, a slice of apple, a grape, a metal object.

Do they float? Which layer do they float on? You could make a chart of your results in a notebook.

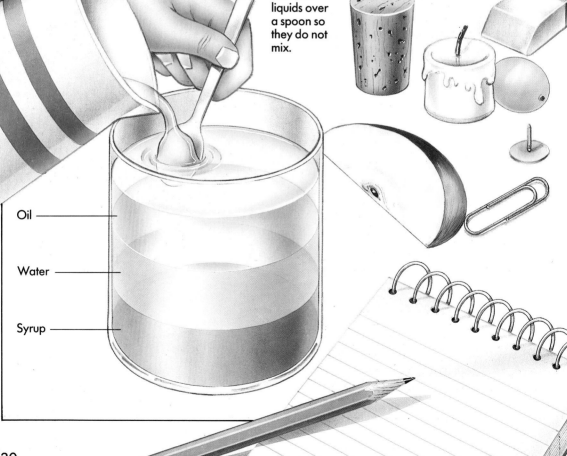

Pour the liquids over a spoon so they do not mix.

Oil

Water

Syrup

The Magic Egg Trick

Salt water is more dense than fresh water, which is why it is easier to float in the sea. You can use this scientific fact to perform a magic trick with an egg.

Equipment: Two glasses, salt, two eggs.

Salt water

Fresh water

Now try this magic trick.
Fill one glass half full of fresh water and one half full of very salty water, as before. Then, very carefully, pour the fresh water into the salt water. Don't let the liquids mix. Gently lower the egg into the water. It should float on the salt water and look as if it is suspended in the middle of the glass by magic!

Mix plenty of salt (about 10 heaped teaspoons) into half a glass of water. Fill the second glass half full of fresh water. Try floating an egg in each glass. You will find that the egg will float in the salt water because it is **less** dense than salt water. But the egg will sink in the fresh water because it is **more** dense than fresh water.

Top of salt water layer.

Water Mixtures

If you mix sugar into tea, it disappears and the tea tastes sweet. This is called **dissolving** and the experiments on these two pages will help you to investigate this process. On pages 34 and 35 you can find out how the dissolved substances can be separated from the water again.

Salt-in-Water Trick

Take a glass full of water and an egg cup full of salt. Do you think you can dissolve all the salt in the water without making the glass overflow?

Try it and see. Sprinkle the salt gently on to the water and use a thin wire to stir it in. When substances dissolve, they do not take up extra space.

Mixing Oil and Water

Water and oil do not mix. Birds keep their feathers waterproof by spreading oil from a special gland onto their feathers. Try mixing oil and water for yourself and see what happens.

1. Put a little cooking oil and water in a jar. Fix the lid on firmly and shake the jar hard. When you put the jar down, the oil and water will separate into two layers.

2. Now add a few drops of washing-up liquid and shake the jar again. This will produce a cloudy mixture.

How it works
The soap in the washing-up liquid breaks up the oil into small drops, which hang in the water and make it look cloudy. This is how washing-up liquid helps to remove grease from plates and saucepans.

Dissolving Tests

Many substances dissolve in water but some do not. Investigate some of these: salt, fine sand, tea leaves, washing soda, bicarbonate of soda, rice, jelly. Stir a small amount of each substance into a jar of water and make a note of what happens. Does it make a difference if the water is warm ?

Make Your Own Stalactites

Stalactites and stalagmites are columns of stone, which form in underground caves. They are made from minerals dissolved in the rainwater that drips slowly from the roofs and walls of caves. As it drips, the water evaporates (see p. 4–5) and leaves the dissolved minerals behind.

Equipment: Two glass jars, woollen thread, washing soda.

1. Fill the two jars with very warm water. Dissolve as much washing soda in each one as you can.

2. Place the two jars in a warm place and put a saucer between them. Twist several strands of woollen thread together. Dip one end of the thread in each jar and let it hang down in the middle. The two solutions should creep along the thread until they reach the middle and then drip onto the saucer.

3. Leave the jars in place for several days and you will see tiny stalactites and stalagmites forming in the centre of the wool. As the water evaporates, a column of crystals forms.

▼ Stalagtites hang down from the roof of a cave; stalagmites grow up from the cave floor.

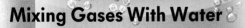

Mixing Gases With Water

- Fizzy drinks contain a gas called carbon dioxide dissolved in them. When you open a can or bottle of fizzy drink, the fizz you can hear and feel is bubbles of the gas escaping.
- Air dissolves in water too. Pumps connected to fish tanks force air into the water so the fishes can breathe.
- Hot water holds less dissolved gas than cold water. As you heat water, the bubbles you can see are bubbles of air escaping into the atmosphere.

How to Make Fresh Water

Sea water is too salty for drinking. But it is possible to remove the salts dissolved in it and make it fit to drink. This is carried out on a large scale at desalination plants, although it is an expensive process. Sea water is heated until it evaporates and the vapour is condensed back to liquid water by passing it over hundreds of pipes that contain cold water. Try making a small amount of fresh water for yourself to see how it is done.

Ask an adult to help you. Take care with hot pans and liquids and don't forget to turn off the heat when you have finished.

Equipment: Salt, water, a clean cup, oven gloves, a saucepan with a lid.

How it works

As the water boils, it evaporates and turns to vapour, which condenses on the cool lid to form drops of liquid water (see pages 6–7). The salt cannot do this and stays behind in the saucepan. So the water you collect from the saucepan lid should not taste salty.

Wait until water is cool before you taste it.

1. Pour water into the saucepan until it is about 5–8 cm (2–3 inches) deep. Mix in lots of salt. Taste it – Ugh!

2. Heat the water until it boils and keep it simmering gently. Put the lid on the saucepan.

3. Use the oven gloves to lift off the lid. Tip the drops of water into the cup. Replace the lid and do this again until you have enough to taste.

Cleaning Water

Most of the water people use for drinking, washing and cooking comes from rivers, lakes or wells. In the richer countries of the world, water is cleaned before and after it is used. The water is first pumped to reservoirs where it is stored until it is needed. Then it travels to a water treatment works where dirt is removed and chlorine is added to kill any harmful germs in the water (see photo). After this clean water has been used by people, the dirty water is carried away in the sewers to a sewage works. There any dirt is removed and special bacteria are added to eat up any harmful germs. The clean water is returned to the rivers again.

Remove the Mud

Here is another way to clean water by removing some of the substances it contains. In this case, the substance to be removed (mud) is not dissolved in the water but floats throughout the water. All you need are two containers and a handkerchief or small towel. Fill one container with muddy water and put it higher than the other container. Place one end of the handkerchief or towel into the muddy water and let the other end hang down into the other bowl.

How it works

The water rises up the narrow air spaces in the cloth by **capillary action** (see pages 14–15) and then trickles slowly down the cloth into the lower container. Mud particles cannot do this and are left behind.

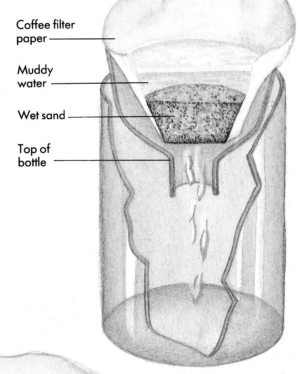

Muddy water

Clear water

Use a pile of books to lift one container higher than the other.

Warning:
Do not drink the water; it may contain harmful germs.

How to Filter Water

This experiment will help you to understand one of the stages in cleaning water at a water treatment works.

Equipment: Muddy water, a plastic bottle, coffee filter paper, some sand, barbecue charcoal (crushed to a powder).

1. Cut the top off the bottle about 8–10 cm (3–4 inches) down from the lid.
2. Turn the top upside down and rest it in the remainder of the bottle. Put in a coffee filter and a layer of wet sand. Then pour some muddy water onto the sand. You will see that it looks a little cleaner as it drips through the filter.
3. You could try to improve your filter by putting a layer of **powdered** charcoal above the sand and then adding another layer of sand above the charcoal. Particles of dirt will be trapped in the layers and this helps to clean the water. The fine particles in the powdered charcoal trap more dirt than the larger grains of sand.

Coffee filter paper

Muddy water

Wet sand

Top of bottle

Warning
Do not drink the water; it may contain harmful germs.

Powdered charcoal

Filter paper

Water for Life

Did you know that at least 65 per cent of your body is water? Or that 95 per cent of a jellyfish is made up of water? All living things have a high percentage of water in their bodies and need water to survive. Many plants and animals spend their whole lives in water. Others survive with very little water.

► In some countries, people have to walk a long way every day to collect water from a well. This well is in an African country called Malawi.

The Ocean Dwellers

Plants and animals that live in the oceans obtain all the air and food they need from the water around them. Some animals hunt for food; others stay put and wait for it to drift past. Microscopic animals floating in the water provide a source of food for many animals, including some of the great whales. These whales have bony plates (called baleen plates) with fringes on the end in their mouths. The fringe strains tiny animals from the sea water. At the bottom of the oceans, it is very cold and dark and no plants can survive. Many of the animals feed on the dead bodies of plants and animals, which drift down from the surface.

Water supports the bodies of plants and animals. You can see this if you compare the appearance of seaweed under the water and in the air.

In air

In water

Water From the Desert

This experiment shows you how to collect water from sand that seems too dry to contain any water at all. You can try it in a sand pit or at the seaside.

Dig a hole about 60 cm (2 feet) deep and put a cup in the centre. Cover the hole with a sheet of plastic so that it dips down in the middle. Weigh the sheet down with a stone and hold the edges down firmly with stones and sand. As the Sun shines, drops of water will slowly form underneath the plastic sheet and run down into the cup.

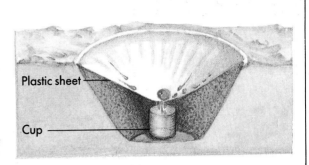

Plastic sheet

Cup

How it works

The heat of the Sun warms the sand under the plastic sheet and some of the moisture in the sand evaporates and then condenses on the plastic (see pages 6–7).

Desert Survival

Plants and animals that live in the desert cope with the lack of water in a variety of ways. Some plants, such as cacti, store water in their stems. Others, including mesquite trees, have deep roots to reach water deep underground. Many plants survive the dry conditions as seeds buried in the desert sand and flower only after a rainstorm. Many desert animals spend the day in underground burrows or rest in the shade. They come out to search for food and water at night, when it is cooler. Some desert animals have to get most of their water from the food they eat.

▲ Look out for water wheels when you are in the countryside. See if you can work out how the water makes the wheel turn round and try to find out what the water power was used for. This water wheel is in the Black Forest region of Germany.

Energy From the Tides

A dam on the estuary of the River Rance in Brittany, France uses the power of the tides to make electricity. The water trapped by the dam is released through 24 special turbines, which can spin in either direction. This means that electricity can be generated both as the tide comes in and as it goes out.

Water Power

The power of moving water has been used for hundreds of years as a source of energy. Water-mills on the banks of fast-flowing rivers used water power to turn stones, which ground wheat into flour. Today, hydro-electric power stations all over the world use the energy of flowing water to produce electricity. The energy of tides and waves can also be used to produce electricity.

Hydro-Electric Power

Hydro-electric power stations use the power of falling water to produce electricity. The water may come from natural waterfalls, such as Niagara Falls, or from the water held back by artificial dams. The water rushes over large wheels called turbines and makes them turn. This drives machines called generators, which produce electricity. You can see how this works in the diagram below.

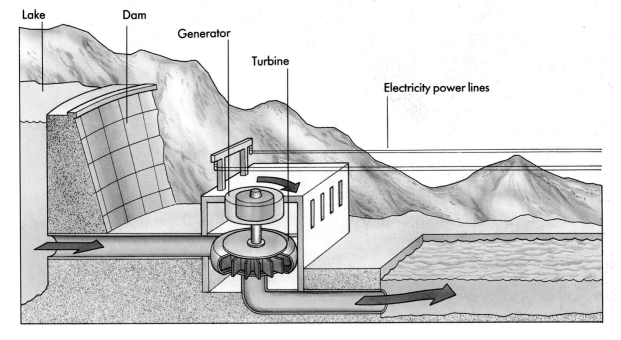

Lake   Dam   Generator   Turbine   Electricity power lines

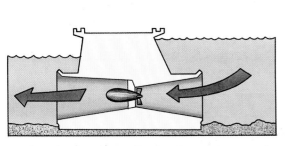

As the tide rises, water flows in from the sea and turns the turbines as it passes into the estuary.

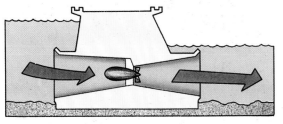

As the tide falls, the water turns the turbines in the opposite direction as it flows back out to sea.

Wave Energy

The movement of the waves can also be used to make electricity. One experimental machine for harnessing wave energy is called the 'nodding boom' or 'duck'. The waves make the 'beak' of each 'duck' nod up and down. This energy is used to produce electricity in small generators inside the 'ducks' themselves.

Index

Page numbers in *italics* refer to illustrations or where illustrations and text occur on the same page.

Editor: Barbara Taylor
Designer: Ben White
Illustrators: Kuo Kang Chen
Peter Bull
Consultant: Terry Cash

Additional Illustrations: Catherine Constable; pages 18–21, 34–37
Cover Design: The Pinpoint Design Company
Picture Research: Jackie Cookson

Photograph Acknowledgements: 4 top ZEFA; 5 bottom right J.Allan Cash; 9 top ZEFA; 10 bottom ZEFA; 12 top right New York State, Commerce Dept, Albany, N.Y.; 16 bottom right Science Museum, London; 17 top left London Fire Brigade; 27 top Port of Rotterdam; 31 top J.Allan Cash; 33 bottom right ZEFA; 34 bottom Thames Water; 36 top, 38 top and bottom ZEFA.

Kingfisher Books, Grisewood & Dempsey Ltd, Elsley House, 24–30 Great Titchfield Street, London W1P 7AD

First published in 1987 by Kingfisher Books
20 19 18 17 16 15 14 13 12 11 10 9
Copyright © Grisewood & Dempsey Ltd 1987

BRITISH LIBRARY CATALOGUING IN PUBLICATION DATA
Walpole, Brenda
Water. – (Fun with science)
1. Water – Juvenile literature
I. Title II. Series
553.7 GB662.3

ISBN 0-86272-290-X

Phototypeset by: Tradespools Ltd., Frome, Somerset
Colour separations by: Scantrans pte Ltd, Singapore
Printed in Hong Kong